Warr Queens

Written by Vanessa York
Illustrated by Xiangyi Mo and Jingwen Wang

Vietnam

Contents

Who Were the Trung Sisters?

Trung Trac and Trung Nhi were two sisters who led the Vietnamese people in a rebellion against their Chinese overlords in A.D. 39. They were strong leaders who were well trained in warfare. They successfully drove the Chinese invaders out of Vietnam, even though it was for only a short time. They are still remembered today for their courage and patriotism. 66

circa A.D. 10	circa 12	circa 29	circa 35
Trung Trac is born in the city of Me Linh, in the Lac province of Vietnam.	Trung Nhi is born.	China sends To Dinh to be the governor of Vietnam.	Trung Trac marries Thi Sach.

Setting the Scene

Vietnam, 2,000 Years Ago

Vietnam was conquered by China in 111 B.C. The Chinese took land and taxes from the Vietnamese people. They also tried to force them to adopt Chinese culture.

There were several uprisings against the invaders, although all of them failed within a year or two. The most successful uprising was led by the two sisters, Trung Trac and Trung Nhi.

CHINA

• Me Linh

VIETNAM

39	39	40	43
Thi Sach is killed by the Chinese governor.	Led by the Trungs, the Vietnamese people rebel.	Trung Trac and Trung Nhi are crowned queens.	Faced with defeat the Trung sisters kill themselves.

Early Life

circa A.D. 20

Trung Trac and Trung Nhi were the daughters of Phong, lord of the city of Me Linh, and his wife, Thoa. The two girls were strong and healthy. They were almost inseparable, and the house rang with their games and laughter from morning until night.

Phong and Thoa had no sons, so they raised their daughters to be leaders. The two girls grew quickly and became experts with weapons, horses, and elephants. They learned about business and about diplomacy, the art of dealing with people. Trung Trac was the better fighter, but Trung Nhi was a better diplomat.

inseparable   not able to be kept apart

Me Linh was a bustling city between two rivers, the Hong (Red) River and the Chay River, in the north of Vietnam. By the time the Trung sisters were born, Me Linh and the land around it had been dominated by the Chinese for about 100 years.

Unlike many societies at that time, Vietnamese society generally saw women as equal to men and gave them many rights. Women could inherit property and become leaders, judges, traders, and warriors.

Today, the memory of the Trung sisters is honored in many Vietnamese temples, including this one in the Me Linh district.

dominate to control or have power over other people

7

Growing Up

As the girls grew older, they became aware of the hardship that the Vietnamese people suffered because of the Chinese overlords' demands for revenue. *Taxes were very high, and many valuable objects were taken as payment. Lord Phong asked Governor Dinh to be more reasonable, but his request was ignored.*

As soon as she was old enough, Trung Trac attended meetings with her father. She saw how greedy Governor Dinh was and how little he cared for the local people. She realized that the Vietnamese could never be free while the Chinese ruled their country.

revenue   the money that a government gets from taxes and other sources

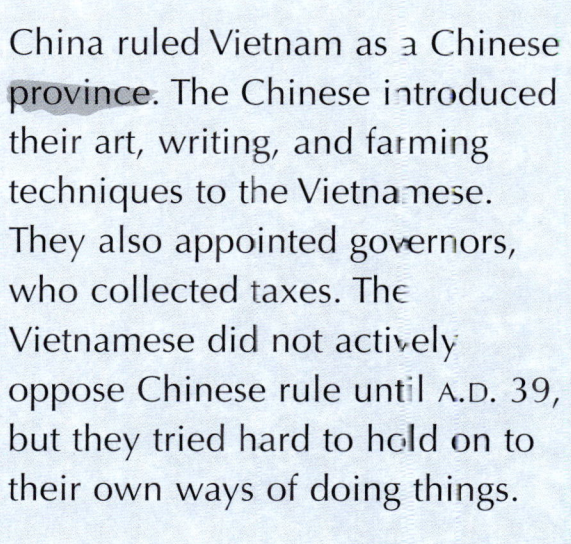

China ruled Vietnam as a Chinese province. The Chinese introduced their art, writing, and farming techniques to the Vietnamese. They also appointed governors, who collected taxes. The Vietnamese did not actively oppose Chinese rule until A.D. 39, but they tried hard to hold on to their own ways of doing things.

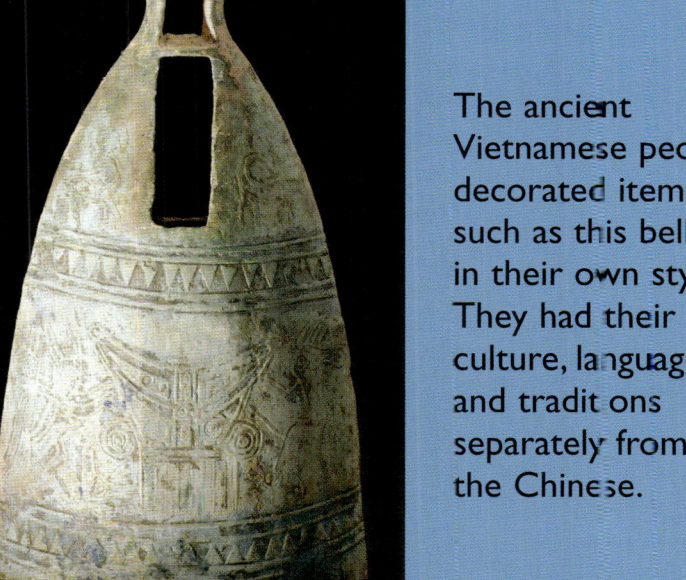

The ancient Vietnamese people decorated items, such as this bell, in their own style. They had their own culture, language, and traditions separately from the Chinese.

province a political region of a country

A Common Cause

One day, Trung Trac attended a meeting with Governor Dinh and the Vietnamese chiefs of the province. At this meeting, she met Thi Sach. They discovered that they had many interests in common. They shared a strong sense of *injustice* over Chinese rule and a desire to see their country free. Soon the two were married.

Together, Trung Trac and Thi Sach often argued with Governor Dinh on behalf of their people. Governor Dinh ignored Trung Trac because she was a woman, but he decided that Thi Sach was a troublemaker. One day, Thi Sach didn't return home. Trung Trac sent people out to look for him. She found out that the governor had ordered him killed.

injustice   unfair treatment of a person or people

10

In A.D. 29, Governor Dinh was given control of Vietnam. The Vietnamese nobility were still allowed to rule their own estates and towns, as long as they paid their taxes and were obedient to Governor Dinh. However, Dinh was the harshest as well as the greediest governor that Vietnam had ever had.

At a traditional Vietnamese wedding, the groom goes to the bride's house for a ceremony with her parents. The bride wears a red gown called an *ao dai*.

Trung Nhi did not know how to comfort her widowed sister. Nothing could lift Trung Trac from her deep despair. Meanwhile, outrage grew among the people of the city. They wanted revenge for Thi Sach's death, and they were also angry about the high taxes. They refused to pay their taxes, and a large crowd took over a police station. Surprised by the suddenness of the attack, the Chinese police put up little resistance.

Encouraged, the people attacked more stations, forcing the police inside to surrender. Then the crowd marched to Trung Nhi and demanded that she lead them in revolt against the Chinese government.

revolt a rebellion against a government or other authority

Governor Dinh had Thi Sach killed as a warning to other rebellious Vietnamese. Thi Sach and Trung Trac had both worked to free their country from China's brutal governor. They were becoming more and more popular with local people, and this worried the Chinese. Their revolutionary ideas were punished harshly.

Chinese officials lived comfortably. They usually traveled by horse and cart. They were even buried with small horse-and-cart models, which were meant to transport them in the afterlife.

Rebellion

A.D. 39

Trung Nhi took some representatives of the people to her elder sister. They urged her to seize the chance they had been waiting for. "Our people are ready to revolt at last!" a farmer told her.

Trung Trac was still mourning the loss of her husband. Although she had long dreamed of rebellion, she felt too sorrowful to fight a battle. Trung Nhi begged her sister. "If we don't get rid of our oppressors now, we never will," she said. At last, Trung Trac agreed to lead her people against the powerful Chinese.

oppressor   a person in power who treats others in a cruel and unjust way

Governor Dinh put most of his energy into making money for himself. He was not a brave man, and he spent little time thinking about strategies for war. He was, therefore, unprepared for an attack.

After the Vietnamese people had successfully taken over several police stations, they realized they might be able to gain even more control. They chose the Trung sisters to lead them.

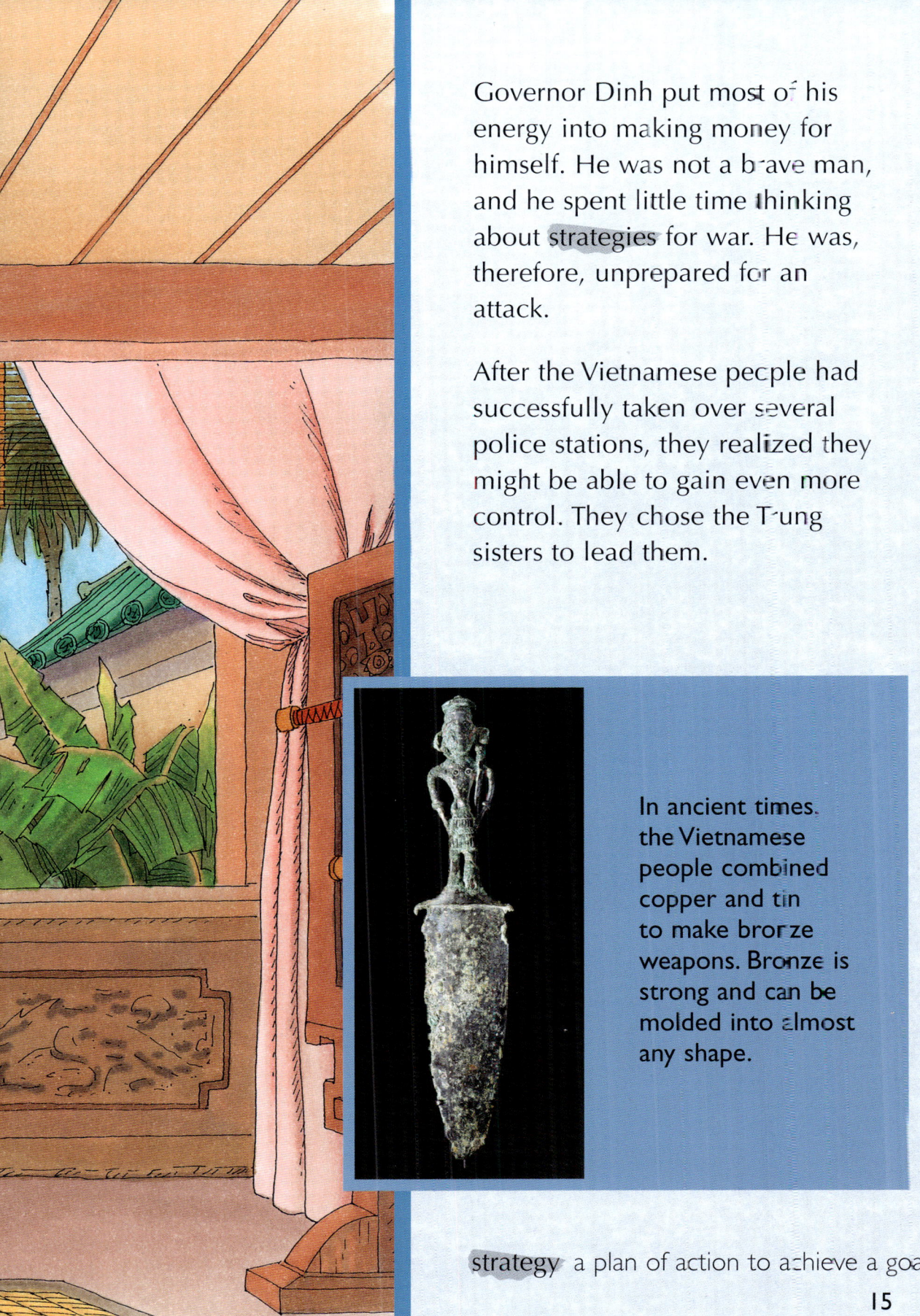

In ancient times, the Vietnamese people combined copper and tin to make bronze weapons. Bronze is strong and can be molded into almost any shape.

strategy a plan of action to achieve a goal

15

Once she had decided to act, Trung Trac organized her troops quickly. Trung Nhi was her second-in-command, and they began training more people to fight. There were many women as well as men in their army.

To win more people over to their cause, Trung Nhi suggested that Trung Trac hunt and kill a fierce tiger that had terrorized a nearby town for years. Trung Trac accomplished this feat easily. Trung Nhi then wrote a *proclamation* on the tiger's skin, calling on the people of Vietnam to rise against their Chinese overlords.

proclamation   a public announcement

> *"First of all, I will avenge my country. Secondly, I will restore the Hung lineage. Thirdly, I will avenge the death of my husband. Lastly, I vow that these goals will be accomplished."*
> —Trung Trac's vow

Trung Trac and Trung Nhi chose 36 women to be generals in their army, and they trained the women personally. The Vietnamese continued to attack the Chinese police stations. Then they attacked the barracks where the Chinese troops were stationed. The Chinese panicked and fled Vietnam.

This ancient Vietnamese ax has a tiger emblem. Tigers were symbols of power, and in those days, killing one was thought to be a sign of bravery. Trung Trac proved herself a worthy leader by killing a tiger that had attacked people.

Queens of Vietnam

Soon the Trung sisters had an army of 80,000 men and women, and they had *liberated* 65 towns. A few of these towns were ruled by Vietnamese lords who would not join the Trung sisters' rebellion, but many tribal lords did fight under their banner.

When Governor Dinh fled, taking with him what was left of his armies, the Trungs took control of their country. Trung Trac and Trung Nhi were declared the queens of Vietnam. They established their royal court in Me Linh.

liberate   to set someone or something free

18

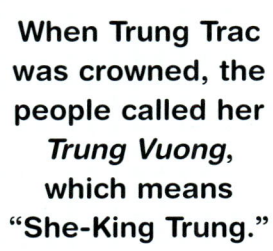

When Trung Trac was crowned, the people called her *Trung Vuong*, which means "She-King Trung."

Governor Dinh shaved his head and fled Vietnam, disguised as a monk. Once he left, the Chinese were no longer in control of Vietnam.

Trung Trac abolished the harsh taxes that the Chinese had imposed on the people. She also started to simplify the system of government, in keeping with traditional Vietnamese values.

Governor Dinh's disguise as a Buddhist monk was certainly ironic. Monks give up their attachment to worldly goods. Dinh's attitude toward life was completely the opposite.

ironic a situation that is the opposite of what you would expect

A Losing Battle

A.D. 42

The Trung sisters did not enjoy peace for long. Eighteen months after they began their rule, China sent a great army to crush the rebellion and recapture the region.

The Chinese army took a stand on the hills above the plains of Lang Bac. The Vietnamese faced them in a position of much less advantage. Frightened by the size of the Chinese army, some of the Trungs' followers deserted them. The Trungs fought fiercely, but they were overwhelmed and forced to retreat. The Chinese once again controlled Vietnam.

desert to abandon someone or something

The Chinese remained in control
of Vietnam for another 900 years,
although there were four more
rebellions during that time.
The second rebellion, in A.D. 248,
was also led by a woman. She
liberated Vietnam for one year.

Kings, queens, and high officials
rode elephants to war. The
elephant gave them a height
advantage and would have
frightened many warriors
on foot or horseback.

National Heroines

In the centuries since their deaths, the Trung sisters have become symbols of national courage. Many temples have been built in their honor. One of the biggest is in Hanoi, the capital of Vietnam. Stories, poems, plays, and even stamps still celebrate the heroism of Trung Trac and Trung Nhi. Every year on February 6, the Vietnamese people honor their memory with ceremonies and festivals.

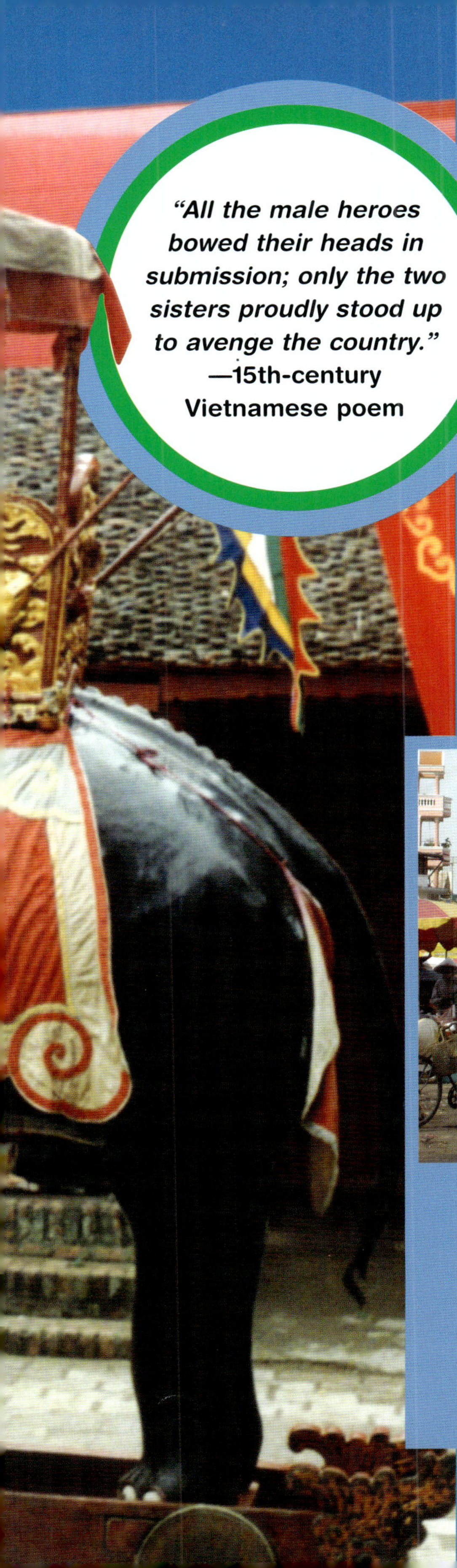

> *"All the male heroes bowed their heads in submission; only the two sisters proudly stood up to avenge the country."*
> —15th-century Vietnamese poem

Why Are They Still Remembered?

- The Trung sisters successfully organized their people to overthrow their oppressors in spite of the odds against them.
- They are symbols of courage and hope.
- They are models of patriotism and of capable women.

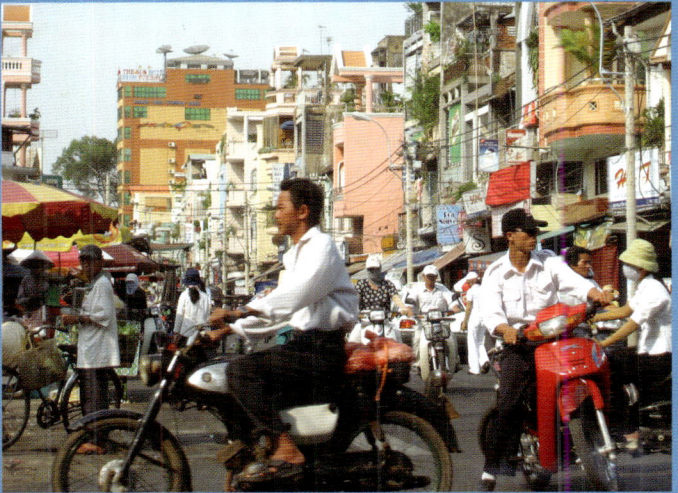

This street in Ho Chi Minh City, Vietnam, is called Hai Ba Trung Street, which means "street of the two Trung sisters."

What If?

The Trung sisters lived 2,000 years ago. They fought hard for the freedom of their country, and for a while, they were successful. What if they had lost their first battle against the Chinese? Do you think people in Vietnam would still remember them and honor them today?

In what ways did Trung Trac and Trung Nhi show courage?

Index

courage being brave